Let it Multiply!

How to Control Your Finances Easily

By: Nolan Myers

9781635011494

PUBLISHERS NOTES

Disclaimer – Speedy Publishing LLC

Speedy Publishing LLC

40 E Main Street, Newark, Delaware, 19711

Contact Us: 1-888-248-4521

Website: http://www.speedypublishing.co

REPRINTED Paperback Edition: ISBN: 9781635011494

Manufactured in the United States of America

DEDICATION

This book is dedicated to you. This will serve as your inspiration to be the master of your own finances.

TABLE OF CONTENTS

Chapter 1- How to Effectively Learn to Save

The general rule of thought is, the earlier an individual starts to put money aside towards saving s, the more likely this said sum will eventually become a rather attractive amount to facilitate some form of comfortable retirement plans. Get all the info you need here.

For most people going into the work force today there is very little possibility of being able to enjoy some sort of pension plans as these plans are becoming more "extinct".

Such pension plan facilities are no longer a requirement or a compulsory addition to an individual's salary deductions. Therefore without such allowances in place for retirement the individual would be wise to start a saving plan to accommodate the retirement phase of his or her life.

Let it Multiply!

Learning to lock in a certain amount as soon as possible towards a savings plan will allow the individual to plan accordingly, thus ensuring this said sum is systematically allotted.

Making this a habit that comes naturally will help to make the entire saving exercise both easy and accepted. It will also allow the individual to work round other financial commitments to ensure the savings contributions are not effected in any way.

Besides this the individual will learn to be disciplined and thus create a comfortable spending habit from a very early on age. The percentage of the savings should also be increased according to the job advancements made.

This would ensure the savings amount becomes healthier which in turn would ensure a more comfortable retirement phase.

Investing in suitable savings plans will also allow the individual to make tax relief claims which should work as an incentive to save even more or provide the funds to invest even more towards a suitable retirement plan.

Saving Method

These are two very powerful savings tools that are becoming more popular as more working adults opt for such plans. The assurance of having money put away for retirement through these secure platforms will encourage those not yet doing so to seriously consider these options.

A 401k plan is basically a scenario where the company the individual is currently working for, offers, as part of its remuneration package a percentage based on the salary amounts to be paid on behalf of the individual, toward this account on a monthly basis.

These amounts are then accumulated plus interest to provide for the retirement phase of the individual. The lock in period for this type of saving plan is also another advantage as the individual will have no access to the amounts in the account until retirement age is reached, thus effectively keeping the money safe from unnecessary seeming important spending sprees for the individual.

IRA investments usually come in two forms which are traditional and Roth. However both are compatible to a retired persons needs as serves as a good investing tool.

The traditional IRA is done in a more independent manner which for some is a better option, as they get to dictate the investment amount and how to invest.

There is also the advantage of the amount being partially tax deductible depending on the plan chosen. The difference here is that there is a possibility of withdrawing some amounts before the actual retirement age but this is then subject to certain taxation issues.

Upon retirement there is also a tax on the amounts withdrawn though it is quite minimal.

For early withdrawal there is also a penalty charged. As for the Roth IRA the similarities between the two are evident however there are also some differences. One of which is the Roth style is not subject to tax deductions upon retirements as the tax is deducted on the amounts are deposited and taken at that time..

Let it Multiply!
Investment

If an individual is only going to depend on a savings plan for retirement, the eventual amounts saved may not be nearly enough to support a comfortable retirement phase as the inflations and value of the money will definitely be lesser as time goes on.

Therefore there is a serious need to look towards investing in other tools that may provide comfortable returns that would add on to the savings plan in place.

The following are some recommendations on other possible areas that should be explored with the intention of creating investment plans for retirement:

Investment planning – this area can provide the individual with platforms where the money works on fetching a better than average interest earnings by planning the investments at the right time and choice. These usually provide with good return on the values over time.

Real estate investment – real estate investments is all about committing funds to entities, such as various forms of properties that will eventually yield suitable income earning revenue for the individual. There may come in the form of rentals, leases and proper deals, where the properties bought can be sold for very good profits.

These are all ways to create suitable savings possibilities.

Bonds and securities investment plans – these can bring about effective investment growth that will eventually contribute toward the funds that can secure a comfortable retirement phase for the individual. The long term investments may come in the form of bonds such as life assurance and death policies. Besides this there are also possibilities investing in government bonds and other entities.

Endowment policies – these are also another very good option to take up in the quest to create a comfortable savings platform to retirement. Is you are paying towards such plans you will create an ideal source on income eventually.

CHAPTER 2- SIMPLE GUIDE ON HOW TO INVEST

With so many options available to make good investments it can be quite confusing for the individual who is not savvy and does not possess the important elements it takes to be a good and sound investor. The various investment opportunities available, also comes with a lot of confusing jargon, that the individual may not be able to relate to, thus causing further confusion and maybe even contributing to some poor judgment calls.

Most people are busy with the everyday routines and distractions, that sparing the time and energy to delve into the mostly confusing financial investment opportunities is really not an option that can be fully explored.

Although some may take the plunge, most would rather engage the services of a reputable financial advisor who would be able to completely concentrate on finding the best investment opportunities for the client. As these financial advisors are more knowledgeable on the various sorts of investment tools available, their opinions would be better accepted. Most financial advisers depend very much on the recommendations of satisfied clients, to expand their portfolios of customers, thus being experienced and good investment advisors is part of their attention grabbing tools.

Financial advisors are also trained to help an individual plan and budget according to their financial capabilities and this can be useful to an individual who is currently not able to enjoy or capitalize, on his or her own financial standing.

Frugal Living

Living frugally does not necessarily mean living in poverty or having to constantly deprive one's self of the finer things in life. Depriving one's self of anything and everything is not what the frugal living lifestyle is all about. In fact it is just the opposite, because with frugal living the individual is able to keep expenses low, pay off debts faster, save and invest comfortably.

The following are explanations on how to "marry" the two factors while still being able to enjoy a fairly pleasant lifestyle that is neither deprivative nor depressing: Learning to be comfortable with smaller size elements that work well and are equally compatible with the individual's lifestyle.

Although it may seem nice to have everything is large sizes, from houses to cars to holidays to spending allowances, with a little bit or knowledge and research anyone can find smaller yet suitably tailor elements that are equally if not better.

Therefore going big always may not only seem a wasteful opulence it can also lead to huge debts.

Let it Multiply!

For some leasing or renting may present a more financially attractive package than actually owning. This is due to the fact that when there is ownership issues involved, all expenses and cost are born by the owner itself, and these hidden costs can be quite substantial.

Therefore with the savings from all these hidden expenses and cost that come from ownership, the individual can look for good investment opportunities that may bring about an even better financial standing.

When it comes to eating expenses, most individuals do not really realize just how much can be saved and how to go about making these adjustments to procure the intended savings. Eating frugally yet healthily is one way of keeping the expenses in check. Taking the trouble to fix meals at home is more cost effective that going out to eat all the time.

Mutual Fund Investment

Recently there has been a lot of interest in this form of investment tool. The mutual fund investment platform presents an attractive alternative to savings toward a comfortable retirement. Besides saving towards retirement there are also other financial goals that can be effectively met through the mutual fund style of investing.

Mutual funds can most time offer the advantage of providing diversified and professional management, but this is done for a fee. As with other forms of investments there is a certain level of risk involved in the dabbling of mutual fund investments.

In some cases if the investment does not pan out as first anticipated or expected, there are fees and taxes incurred that will make the whole exercise quite disadvantages and also end up being the cause of the diminishing in fund returns.

Therefore in the quest to ensure optimum benefits are derived from this type of investment there has to be some level of understanding, by the investor about the downsides and the upsides of the mutual fund investing tool.

The prospective investor should have some sound knowledge about how the mutual funds work, what factors should be considered when researching for possible investments, how to avoid pitfalls and problems and any other information that might have an impact on the choices made.

Some of these factors may include the degree of risks involved both in the long term and short term style for the mutual funds chosen, the strategies involved in making such decisions and how to ensure these decisions are made based on sound knowledge, the fees and expenses that are normally incurred through the investing process and some of the terms and labels used to describe the various levels and connotations linked to the mutual fund itself.

The main idea behind choosing the mutual fund investment is to ensure the retirement plan is well served by this form of savings.

Making money and losing money today can be a life changing or life threatening experience. For some the challenge of being able to dictate their own financial journey is important, while for others a little help may be not only necessary but perhaps even compulsory. Here is when the services of a financial adviser could prove to be an advantage worth taking.

CHAPTER 3- YOUR FINANCES AND YOUR BUDGET PLAN

Budgeting may not necessarily be all about curbing all spending powers. It is only a suggested method of spending, that is both wise and that will keep the individual from falling into an all consuming debt ridden situation. Get all the info you need here.

Perhaps the first and most important act to commit to is the detailed tracking exercise of the expenses for the individual monthly commitments.

Creating a tracking system from the close scrutiny of bills collected over a three month period will help give the individual an idea of the general commitments to date.

By having this clearly listed and detailed the individual will be able to design a suitable budget that can be easily followed without the need to be too constrictive.

This budgeting exercise can take into account all expenses such as fixed commitments, periodic commitments, occasional treats and any other types of usual expenses calculated on a monthly basis.

Settings goals is also another type of personal budgeting element that should be included as a form of incentive to the individual. It is also a way to create discipline that will help the individual prepare for bigger commitments in the future. Setting goals will also help the individual have a better perspective on the future possibilities of investment opportunities.

The act to creating and adhering to a personal budget plan can also help the individual be disciplined in other fields too. This may contribute positively in other areas, such as job commitments, family commitments, retirement plans, investments and any other area that may require the same discipline that produces successful results always.

It will also help the individual to make wiser judgment calls, thus ensuring the possibility of getting in debts be kept at a minimum or even eliminated altogether.

The Future

The following are some steps that can be considered in pursuit of time goal:

Educating one's self on the various different personal investment schemes would be one way of going about securing the future of an individual's personal income.

There are many types of investments that can earn the individual a comfortable amount of profits that can be used as a source of income in the future.

Let it Multiply!

Personal savings plans can also contribute to future income possibilities. However if this plan is not enforced in a committed fashion where access to the funds put away are either limited or nonexistent, then this style of savings will not benefit or be suitable as a future income source.

This is due to the fact that the accessibility will encourage the individual to make withdrawals frequently based on excuse possible.

Having a diversified portfolio of financial investments will also ensure the risk levels are kept to a minimum and that future income projected can be enjoyed.

Choosing long term investment tools are better, as they popularly provide better earning possibilities as compared to short term investment. These may include government bonds, insurance policies, bonds from reputable agencies and establishments.

Being able to accurately access financial investments against the primary risk tolerance of an individual is also something that should be given due consideration.

There is little point in starting an investment portfolio if the ability of service such investments are either nonexistent or unreliable.

All the above suggestions should also be calculated with the relevant tax incurring ratios that should ideally still make the investment worth venturing into.

Be Committed on Your Budget Plan

Following a budget plan is not impossible to do if the right tools and mindset is in place. There are a few true and tried methods that can help an individual design and successfully stick to the budget plan.

The following are some recommendations as to how this can be achieved:

The first and most important act to exercise is the recording of all income and expense for the month. This should be diligently done over a period of at least three months consecutively.

Once these detailed itemized incoming and outgoing points are clearly recorded, then follow up measures can be incorporated into the budget plan to start the process that ensures the individual is well equipped to handle and stick to the plan drawn up.

There are several tools available that can help the individual in this style of tracking.

The next step would be to record only the income and very necessary expenses such as commitments towards loans, insurances, education payments and any others.

Ideally these should be calculated as a yearly expense and then divided to fit into the monthly expenditure plan. This will help the individual have a complete overview of his or her yearly commitments thus providing the means to make such payment in a more disciplined and affordable way.

At the end of the above exercises, it is hoped that the income is greater than the committed expenses. If this is found to be so, then the individual can enjoy the leeway of adding on other expenses that are not deemed necessary or vital to the healthy existence of the individual financial position.

Let it Multiply!

These may include little indulgences such as an occasional expensive meal or personal treat. This will encourage the individual to stick to the budget planned as the possibility of ever being in debt is kept at bay.

Keep Track

Any budget is only as effective as the real time notations that are updated periodically. Having the correct assisting tools will help to make the process of spreadsheet budgeting and date shifting effective.

All spending both immediate and future is usually noted on the spreadsheet but this is not always fixed as adjustments are made accordingly as they unfold. The following are some of the tools and methods used to keep the spreadsheet updated:

Perhaps the most basic tools are the simple jotting down of information on paper to be entered into the spreadsheet when the periodic updating exercise is done.

There are also a lot of money management websites that can help to specifically assist in the money management program. These programs keep track of the all the accounts information which may include saving and other money generating accounts, and then make the necessary adjustments to display useful information for future budgeting.

With the help of the spreadsheet budgeting style, the individual is able to clearly note all payments and commitments at a glance. This is very helpful when trying to decide on the importance tagged to the payments.

If there are credit cards outstanding amounts the spreadsheet will help to highlight the cards that most need attention and if funds permit more money can be focused on paying the debts that have the highest interest rates.

The date shifting done on the information furnished by the spreadsheet will help create a better avenue of clearing the commitments that are either prioritized or cost more in terms of interest accrued. In some way the clarity of the figures shown in this way will create the urgency for the individual to focus on making the relevant payments in its priority form.

It will also give the individual a clear overview of his or her financial status both in the present and in the future if the necessary information is well documented and allocated.

CHAPTER 4- FRUGAL LIVING WHILE HAVING FUN

With careful planning and an income that does not fluctuate too much it is possible to be able to enjoy life in the present without having to chalk up a lot of debts. All it really takes is a little planning and discipline.

The following are some recommendation on how to go about this exercise:

Going on a vacation does not necessarily have to be done in opulent style. Look for alternatives that are similar and equally exciting that will fit into a budget that is available is a better way to plan and enjoy while all the time being firm about keeping within the budget.

The ability to plan within the budget will ensure no unnecessary debts are accumulated thus possibly creating the space to future better holidays, since the current one did not end up burdening the individual with debts that would have to be serviced along after the holiday is over.

Indulging periodically is also advised provided the exercise does not cost as exorbitant amount that will keep the individual in debt long after the enjoyment passes. However total abstinence can also negatively affect the individual as it may cause sudden over indulgence.

Looking for the best deals can not only be fun but also constitute to huge savings possibilities.

Learning to source for items in less convention ways such as garage sales and closing down sales will allow the individual to find items that are not overly prices and yet suited to the current needs. The latest platform that is fast gaining popularity is the online trading style where items are often bought for very low prices indeed.

Focusing on working on side incomes to help pay for indulgences is also another way to enjoy without incurring unnecessary debts. Taking on odd jobs and small project with the intention of using the money for a little pleasure is quite an encouraging tool to go by.

Frugal Household Budget

Most people assume household budgets only consist of immediate expenses incurred within a month that are household expense related. However a complete household budget realistically takes into account all incoming and outgoing funds within the said household on an ideally yearly basis.

Let it Multiply!

The following are some of the areas that are not conventionally addressed but should be done in the quest to have a complete household budget:

There should be a clear and accurate spreadsheet done on the house hold income. This is necessary when there are multiple sources of income, thus creating the need to have such details noted clearly.

There would also be a need to list the mandatory payments that are done within the monthly commitments. If there are any payments that are made in a fashion other than the usual monthly commitments, these payments have to be averaged out and included in the monthly commitment household budget.

Allotments should also be made for discretionary spending which usually covers any and all categories. The allotment should be of a comfortable amount without being over indulgent. This is to ensure there is still some level of discipline and control encompassing the household budget.

Savings are also to be included especially if they are in the context of being part of a commitment towards some sort of plan.

These may include savings for retirement, savings for emergency funds, savings for educational funds and any other long term style commitments that can fluctuate in its committed amounts for payment.

If there are any debts to be cleared, then the payments towards these should also be part of the household budget records. The payments for such existing debts will only be added on for the duration it takes to pay off such platforms.

Tips to Stick on Your Budget Plan

For some people planning a budget is a fairly easy task to carry out, the ability to stick to the planned budget outlined is where the challenge starts. This challenge has often caused many individual to fail or falter in some way.

The following are some tips to help keep this negative possibility from happening:

Drawing up a budget that is both realistic and clear is a good start to make. With this budget the individual is able to have something tangible to focus on and actually be aware of where the incoming and outgoing funds are heading.

Tracking the spending style will give the individual a better overview of how and where the money is being spent. For most this may be a surprisingly eye opening experience as most people don't keep track of the details of their spending habit and are therefore not really aware of just how frivolous some of the purchases made are.

Thus this tracking will help bring some semblance of sanity back into the spending style of the individual and hopefully curb further unnecessary indulgences.

Making it a habit to only use cash for any purchases whether small or large is something that should be adopted immediately. When there is an actual exchange of cash the transaction makes a bigger impact on the individual mindset.

One of the most effective methods to ensure a budget is consistently adhered to is to avoid putting one's self in a situation where the temptation to spend is hard to control. This would mean

Let it Multiply!
cutting down on window shopping sprees and other frivolous indulgences, until the individual is strong enough to do so without actually having to spend on anything. In some more drastic cases the individual may even have to resort to changing the circle of friends he or she hangs out with, if the said group prioritizes activities like shopping and other equally costly indulgences.

CHAPTER 5- GET OUT OF DEBT AND CONTROL YOUR FINANCES

Depending on your particular situation, there are different approaches to getting out of debt. Let's review them now so you can decide which approach will work better for you, based on where you are financially right now.

If you have been paying your bills on time and have a good credit record (and want to keep it in good standing), and you are working or have a monthly income, then you can follow the plan outlined in Part 2. Credit Counseling or Debt Settlement will not be a good choice for you.

If your accounts are past due and you cannot make the payments, then Credit Counseling (also commonly known as Debt Management or Debt Consolidation) or Debt Settlement might be a good choice for you. You can go to Part 3 for more information on these services.

Let it Multiply!

It's important to note that there is no magic bullet that will work for every debt situation. But keep in mind that in many cases, money problems are NOT the result of financial issues but rather a result of how we think.

This may sound esoteric to some people, but when you think about it you will realize that it is true. For example, take any self-made millionaire, somebody that went from poverty to millionaire by himself or herself. If you were to take all their money away, do you think they can make it back? You bet! The reason is that they have a different set of beliefs about what is possible in life, they think differently than most people.

And when you consider that most people that won the lottery lost it all within just a couple of years, then you can see that how we think and what we believe is possible for us makes all the difference in the world.

I don't believe in luck. I don't believe that we are like a leaf in the wind that goes where the wind blows, with no control whatsoever over what is possible. I used to think that way, but not anymore. I believe that we are all in charge of our lives and in charge of our destinies. And I invite you to try this approach in your life, and discover that in reality, you truly are in charge of your destiny. Anything is possible for you, no matter how the economy is doing or what is going on around you.

This is the reason I included the section about how to change your limiting beliefs in this book. Even if you manage to get out of debt without changing your beliefs about what is possible for you, then there is a very high chance that you may get back in debt in the near future. And I sincerely want you to live a successful, happy life that I believe is your birthright.

There is so much abundance around us all the time, yet we fail to appreciate it. Instead, we are taught from an early age that all supplies are limited. Limited jobs, limited opportunities, limited money, limited everything! Then no wonder when we analyze our belief systems -see Part 4- all kinds of limiting beliefs start popping up that we never knew we had, but have been guiding everything we did in our lives since we were little kids.

I sincerely want you to become debt-free as soon as possible, because I believe that being in debt is being in financial slavery. It limits everything you do in your life: whether you will send your kids to private or public school and the education they will receive, the area of town and the house you will live in, even the medical insurance you will get! When you are in a good financial situation, you have many more choices available to you. Living in poverty is NOT the solution to the world's problems.

Now it's time to begin your journey. If you are ready to become debt free and live a financially stress-free life, turn the page over to Part One, where I discuss what credit is and how it can either destroy you or make you rich, depending on how you use it. You will learn what banks and financial institutions don't want you to know...

How credit cards work

If you want to eliminate your credit card debt you have to understand what credit is.

In case you haven't figured it out yet, the credit system works against you, unless you are prepared.

Let it Multiply!

And since it is an unfair game, you need to know the rules. Once you know how credit works, how compound interest works, you can start using it to your advantage, instead of being a victim of it.

Here are some facts you need to know.

In 2005, a record 6 billion "pre-approved" credit card offers were mailed to consumers. By comparison, only 10 years before, in 1995, 2.7 billion offers were mailed out.

These offers usually carry a "low introductory" rate which is "fixed" for a set number of months. But, once you read the fine print, you find out that in reality that "fixed" rate can change at any time, and for any reason. What follows was taken from an offer I recently received from Chase Bank.

"Rates, Fees and terms may change: We reserve the right to change the terms of your account (including the APRs) at any time, for any reason, in addition to APR increases that may occur for failure to comply with the terms of your account" (underlying is mine)

So you may be thinking you are getting a great deal, when in reality they can change the rules whenever they want.

Unfortunately, you cannot beat the system. They write the rules to their advantage and we must comply. Every year, credit card companies, banks and financial institutions spend millions and millions of dollars lobbying Congress to make sure laws are passed that benefit them, not consumers.

You simply cannot compete.

The good news is that you don't need to beat the system; you just need to understand it.

Pre-approved offers are mailed to anyone on a list that a credit card company purchases (usually from the Credit Bureaus), and does not mean that you will definitely get a credit card. They are inviting you to apply, but they are targeting their mailings towards consumers who are more likely to respond and qualify for a card.

If you do not want to receive any more offers, you can call (888)567-8688 to request that Credit Bureaus not include your file in any pre-approved / promotional lists. I encourage you to opt-out, if (for no other reason) to minimize the chances of identity theft.

If you prefer to contact the Bureaus directly, write to the following addresses and tell them you want to opt-out of pre-approval screening:

Equifax Options:

P O Box 7401243 - Atlanta, GA 30374-0123 (800)556-4711

Experian Consumer Opt Out

701 Experian Parkway - Allen, TX 75013 (800)353-0809

TransUnion

Attn: Marketing Opt Out – PO Box 97328 – Jackson, MS 39288-7328

(800) 680-7293

Let it Multiply!

There are several more practices that have become more common in the last few years.

One of them is the "Grace Period", which is the number of days you have to repay your purchase before you are charged interest. Many cards have reduced the grace period from 30 days down to 21 days. With a 21-day grace period you have less time to pay for your purchases in full, and a better chance of paying interest than before. And, if the amount is not paid in full, interest is charged from the date of purchase, not the day you started financing it.

Another practice is the addition of the over-the-limit fee. Many consumers would expect their credit card to be declined if a transaction would put the card over their credit limit. But, increasingly, credit card companies are allowing these transactions to go through, and then slapping consumers with an over-the-limit fee of $20, $25 or more.

Late fees are escalating too, adding $30 to $50 to your credit card bill. Not to mention that your interest rate skyrockets. I personally know someone in New York who sent his payment in late, and his interest rate went from 9% to 29% the following month. This is very common.

There is also the Foreign Transaction fee that you get hit with when withdrawing your money from an ATM outside of the States. Keep that in mind next time you travel.

Simply withdrawing money from an ATM that doesn't belong to the bank means you are going to be hit with two fees. One fee that is charged by the bank that owns the ATM and another fee that is charged by your bank (not all banks will charge this fee, but most will). Withdrawing $20 from another bank's ATM could result in $4 to $6 in fees. How many times a year do you withdraw money from other bank's ATMs?

There are way too many fees to list here, but you get the idea.

Are you asking yourself what you can do to protect yourself?

There are a number of things you can do.

First, you need to check your credit card statements every month. Believe it or not, most people do not check their statements. Check not only your credit card statements but also your checking account and your savings account statements. Look for any errors.

Look for fees, and see if they are correct. If you see any over-the-limit or late fees, call the company and ask (politely) if they can waive them. They will usually waive them, but if you are late again or over the limit again, they may not do it a second time.

Be very careful when mailing your payments. Send them at least 10 days before the due date to avoid late fees. Or set it up so the balance is deducted from your checking or savings account automatically. Contact your bank to find out how to do it.

You can also (and I encourage you to do this) call your credit card companies and ask for a reduction of your interest rate. This may be a little harder to get, but if they don't want to do it, don't despair. Call again in a couple of weeks, and ask again. In Part 2 you can read a script you can use when you call.

Let it Multiply!
What is compound interest?

This is the most important concept to understand if you plan to stay debt free forever.

And for you to understand exactly how it works, I'll ask you a question: What would you rather have, a million dollars in cash right now, or one penny today, two pennies tomorrow, four pennies the next day, eight pennies the next one and so on for the next 30 days?

Most people would choose the million dollars, and it is a good choice, I mean, who wouldn't want a million dollars? However, the second option is much better. Look at the following table to see the power of compound interest in action:

Day 1: $.01

Day 2: $.02

Day 3: $.04

Day 4: $.08

Day 5: $.16

Day 6: $.32

Day 7: $.64

Day 8: $1.28

Day 9: $2.56

Day 10: $5.12

Day 11: $10.24

Day 12: $20.48

Day 13: $40.96

Day 14: $81.92

Day 15: $163.84

Day 16: $327.68

Day 17: $655.36

Day 18: $1,310.72

Day 19: $2,621.44

Day 20: $5,242.88

Day 21: $10,485.76

Day 22: $20,971.52

Day 23: $41,943.04

Day 24: $83,386.08

Day 25: $167,772.16

Day 26: $335,544.32

Day 27: $671,088.64

Day 28: $1,342,177.28

Let it Multiply!
Day 29: $2,684,354.56

Day 30: $5,368,709.12

This is the magic of compound interest. A penny doubled every day may not seem like much, but the compounding factor is incredible. In fact, Albert Einstein has been quoted as saying "The most powerful force in the universe is compound interest."

As you can see in the table above, a penny doubled every day gives you over $5,000,000 in just 30 days. This is how powerful compound interest is. And this is what credit card companies are using against you.

When you make charges on your credit card, you pay interest on any balance you carry (balance would be any unpaid amount on your credit card statement). This interest is calculated not only on the initial principal but also the accumulated interest of prior periods.

Compound interest can really hurt you, especially if you are making the minimum payment on each of your credit cards. When you carry a balance, compound interest is calculated daily, which means every day interest is added to your balance. If you pay the minimum payment on a credit card, you are only making the bank richer.

To show you compound interest in action, consider that if you have a credit card with $5,000 balance at 18% a year, and you were to pay only the minimum payment (let's say it's 3% of your balance), it would take you 199 months to pay it off! (Assuming that the rate doesn't change and you never use your card again). So your account will be paid off in exactly 199 months (over 16 years!) and you will have paid $4,698.46 in interest. This is insane. This is what banks don't want you to know. Send them only the minimum payment and they will love you forever.

How home mortgage loans work

If you own your own home you may not even think of your mortgage as debt. You may even believe that the house is really yours. You need to understand how mortgage loans work if you want to be truly debt-free.

Home mortgages operate the same way that credit cards do. The difference is that mortgage companies will never say that the interest on their loans is compounded daily (maybe on their fine print, buried among hundreds of pages that you sign at closing). But now that you understand how compound interest works, you may start to realize that it only makes sense to pay off your mortgage as soon as possible.

Most people just assume that the interest on their mortgage is simple interest. When they get a 6% interest rate, they think that the interest they pay will be 6% of the total amount they financed, calculated yearly. This is what I found out after talking to my clients. But nothing could be further from the truth. In reality, if you paid off your whole mortgage in one year, then yes, the interest rate would be 6% (well, actually a little more because of the compounding effect, but I'm trying to illustrate a point here). But if it is paid over 30 years, then the actual interest rate is well over 100%! Think about it! You could buy more than 2 houses with the same money!

One of them is the so called "Interest Only" loans. Basically you only pay the interest portion of the payment, deferring the difference (thereby accumulating interest, which is added to your account). It means that you are not only NOT paying down the balance of your loan, but you are also adding more interest (you are adding interest to the balance you didn't yet pay).

If property values are going up, then it may not be a bad loan in some specific cases (i.e., buying a house with the intention of selling it in a few months); however, in a declining market it is financial suicide. The only way somebody would benefit from an Interest Only mortgage loan is if they were sending some money to be applied towards the principal every month and the interest rate is substantially lower than they had before (if they are refinancing). On purchases it was a good option when houses were appreciating very fast, as was the case in many parts of the country not too long ago, but obviously very risky. In today's market, it's definitely not an option to consider.

The riskiest mortgage loans available are called Option ARM (Adjustable Rate Mortgage) or Pick A Pay loans. Every month, you get to pick which payment (out of four) you will send to the mortgage company. This is a good option for professionals or business owners whose income fluctuates sharply from month to month, but definitely NOT for most people.

With option 1 you send less than that month's interest (which means, the difference is added to the balance, collecting more interest.) For example, let's take a $200,000 loan with a Fully Amortizing rate (the real rate that would pay off the loan in 30 years) of 7.683% and a minimum payment rate of 1.25%. The option one payment will be $666.50 (deferring $614 of the interest that was due that month, which automatically is added to the balance and starts collecting interest)

With option 2, you send only the interest for that month (which means, you are not paying down the balance, or explained differently, it's as if you were like "renting" the house! Following the previous example, you would send $1,280.60 for that month, but the balance is not paid down.

With option 3, you send the regular payment (principal and interest) calculated over 30 years. In this example, it will be $1,423.58.

And with option 4 you send the regular payment calculated over 15 years instead of 30, but it will be obviously substantially higher. Following our example that payment would be $1,874.88

Can you guess which payment most people usually send?

I have seen mortgage statements from banks where the option that is highlighted in the payment coupon (or in big, bold letters) is always the minimum payment (option 1). This leads people to believe that's the payment they should send, and many people send just that. One of my clients added $60,000 to his mortgage loan in just 2 ½ years without realizing what was going on. In my experience, many people were not well informed when they were offered these loans.

Option Arm loans can spell trouble, especially when property values decline and home owners owe more than their house is worth. To add insult to injury, when people refinance they discover that the interest rate is always higher on an Option Arm loan than on a 30-year fixed loan! Fortunately, these types of loans are not as popular in the US right now as they were in the early 2000's.

As you can see, ignorance is not bliss, is expensive.

Let it Multiply!

Many people believe that paying off their mortgage is a bad financial decision, and they have two arguments to back up this position. I respect both arguments, but I do not agree with either one. The first argument is that a home mortgage has tax benefits (since mortgage interest can be deducted from your taxes); the second is that since the interest on a mortgage is usually low (around 4 to 6% in the last few years depending on many factors like your credit, etc), you will benefit by making regular payments to your mortgage lender and investing your discretionary income elsewhere, as long as the interest on your investment is higher than the interest on your mortgage.

Let's look at both arguments. As far as the mortgage interest being tax deductible, what it really means is that if you pay, let's say, $10,000 in mortgage interest in a given year, you will save $2,500 in taxes (if you are at a 25% bracket; it would be even less money if you are at a lower bracket!). Think about this for a moment. Does it really make financial sense to you? Paying the bank $10,000 to get back $2,500? If you are like me, it will not make any sense at all. It makes more sense to pay off the mortgage, and once it's paid off, you get to KEEP the $10,000 (or whatever you would have paid in interest) as disposable income or as investment money.

As far as investing your money somewhere else that could give you a higher return (higher than your mortgage interest), let me offer the following facts to you: whatever interest you pay on your mortgage, will be the GUARANTEED interest you will make by paying it off (or paying it down). You cannot guarantee the performance of any other investment, as you probably already know. Market conditions fluctuate and could affect your investments; however, paying off your 6% mortgage is a guaranteed 6 % "return".

And let's face it, most people, including myself, are not keen investors. Many will have a Mutual Fund or retirement account that they rarely review, and investing does take a lot of planning and research.

Without proper planning and research you could be "throwing darts" at your financial future. When you consider this option, then paying off your mortgage early does make financial sense due to its simplicity and high return. However, if you are a keen investor, then it may make sense not to pay off your mortgage and invest your discretionary income somewhere else.

In the next part, I will show you a way to pay off ALL your debt, including your mortgage, in record time. This method is not about refinancing your home, it is not about debt consolidation, nor is it about debt settlement. It is based on a surprisingly simple (and incredibly powerful) formula that will give you the financial freedom you and your family deserve. This system will work even if you are under a debt consolidation program or if you have student loans.

CHAPTER 6- SIMPLE GET-AWAY-FROM-DEBT PLAN

If you are ready to become debt-free, here is an effective, proven strategy that will help you get out of debt in an organized way. Following the step-by-step plan will get you out of debt in record time.

Step 1- You have to absolutely, totally, 100%, commit yourself to getting out of debt - and commit yourself to following your plan, no matter what happens.

This may seem obvious, but the only way you are going to succeed is if you are 100% committed to your debt elimination plan. Anthony Robbins, well known motivational speaker, says that it's in the moments of decisions that our destinies are shaped. Decide TODAY you are going to make it happen. Do not take this step lightly. You will not succeed unless you commit yourself. It may help to get a buddy to keep you on track.

If you ask a successful dieter how they lost the weight and kept if off, they will tell you that it was not by starving themselves, but by committing to a sensible plan. It is that commitment that gets you back on the horse if you fall off the wagon.

Step 2- Stop charging your credit cards as of today!

Your main goal right now is to get out of debt as soon as possible. So you must cut your spending. I know this is tough to do, but you have to cut your credit cards. (Keep one in case of an emergency.) If you are truly committed, stop reading and start cutting. To get out of debt, you will need to change your habits. Your old habits will not work!

The sacrifices you make now will have an incredible benefit in the long term. From now on, if you cannot pay cash for something, don't buy it.

Step 3- Find out where your money is going.

You need to know exactly where your money is going and what your expenses are.

You can use a program like Quicken, AceMoney Lite (free), or similar software to track your money. Use a notepad, a pen and calculator if you don't have a computer.

You must write down ALL your expenses so you can determine exactly where your money is going. Carry with you a piece of paper where you can write down all your cash expenses. They are usually the hardest to track but add up very quickly. Did you buy candy and a soda when you filled up your tank? Write it down.

Let it Multiply!

Once you know where your money is going, look for places where you can "trim" your expenses. Some common examples are:

-Eating lunch out: at $8/day, it is around $200 per month. Some people spend $10 or $12 every day on lunch. Bag your lunch a few times a week.

-Going to Starbucks twice a week: if you only spend $6 a week, it would amount to $25 a month. Maybe you could skip it every now and then?

-Cable TV: Maybe you spend $80/month or more, when you could be paying $40 to $60 by eliminating channels you seldom watch.

-Occasional fast food: $25/week would mean $100/month.

-Magazine subscriptions you seldom read: Cancel them! Same with newspapers, music services, etc.

-Enjoy movies and popcorn at home instead of going out.

-Use coupons for groceries and buy store brands. Don't be tempted to buy something you don't need just because it's on sale. Also, beware of "bargains". If you are the type of person who is attracted to a "Sale" sign as if by a magnet, be aware that they are responsible for much impulse spending.

- Shop at consignment stores & discount stores like Ross or Marshalls (their clothes are usually good quality and people won't notice!)

- Cut down (or eliminate) sodas and snacks. They only make you fat, anyway.

- Eat frozen pizza at home instead of ordering out.

- Use your creativity! Where else could you save money? Remember, you do need to change your lifestyle if you want to make it happen.

- Call two or three car insurance companies and get new quotes. If you can lower your insurance payments through another company, then go ahead and switch! I saved over $600 a year with a 5 minute phone call.

Step 4- Develop a budget.

Consider this: most people spend more time planning a 3-day weekend than they do planning their life. By making a budget, you are committing yourself to getting out of debt, in writing. Use the budget spreadsheet you will find at the end of this book (under Resources) to prepare your budget.

Step 5- Make a list of ALL your creditors (credit cards, department stores, etc) and call them.

You are going to ask them to lower your rate. This has worked amazingly well for many people, including myself. Here is a simple script you can use: "Hi, my name is [Your Name]. I am a good customer, but I have received several offers in the mail from other credit card companies with lower interest rates.

I would like to see if you could lower the rate on my card, as it is a little high". If they say no, then say something like "I would hate to have to switch to another company after being with you for __ years… could you please check again, or could I please talk to your supervisor?" You can also ask to eliminate any fees they may have charged you recently (late fees, yearly fees, etc).

Let it Multiply!

If your credit card company doesn't want to lower your rate, just try again a few days later. You can also say things like "What can you do to help me out?" or "Can you do any better?" For this strategy to work, you have to be polite, but firm. Never threaten, raise your voice or get angry.

Step 6- Open a savings account if you don't have one, and deposit money in it every month.

You have to pay yourself first. This is how you will start building wealth, and it will also be your emergency fund. Every time you get paid, deposit some money in your savings account.

You need to consider two things:

1- Treat it just like any other bill. Deposit money every month, even if it's only $25. Deposit more when you can. Once you make it a habit, this account will grow very quickly;

2- NEVER withdraw money from this account (unless, of course, you have a real emergency that you cannot cover with your income). If you do make a withdrawal, make sure you "pay yourself back" as soon as possible. Hold a garage sale, sell stuff you no longer need, do whatever it takes to replenish the money you took out, AS SOON AS POSSIBLE. Otherwise, let it grow at least for a few years. Once you are debt-free, you can use this money as a down payment for a house, or any other investment. This is critical! Note: a birthday present is NOT an emergency. The idea is to have money in case you need to repair your car, for example, so you don't deviate from your debt elimination plan.

Step 7- Fill out the debt elimination chart, and put the Debt Elimination Program into practice right away.

You will find a copy of the debt elimination chart at the end of this book. You will need it for this exercise. During your Debt Elimination Program you will be focusing on one account at a time and making minimum payments on all others. This is crucial to your success.

When you send an extra $40 to a credit card company, an extra $25 with your car payment and an extra $20 to another account, you are only diluting your efforts. If you tackle many accounts at once, you may feel like you are not accomplishing much because you don't see tangible results. And you will feel discouraged. With this program, you will be focusing on one account at a time until it's paid off. In this example, you will send an extra $85 to one account instead of $40, $25 and $20 to three different accounts.

Now proceed to fill out the debt elimination chart as explained below to determine the order in which the accounts will be paid off.

Look at the chart below as you follow along. The concept is very simple: You will determine the order in which your accounts will be paid off based on a simple formula, and you will pay off one account at a time.

By now you should have determined how much extra money you can dedicate every month to your Debt Elimination Program (we'll call it your "Power Payment"). If possible, I strongly recommend you dedicate 10% of your income as your "Power Payment". For some people this will be easy, for others it may be a little harder. Try to do it at least until you have paid off a few accounts.

As an example, we will use Jonathan and Tracy's chart, from San Diego. They are using $400 as their Power Payment. Their

Let it Multiply!

combined yearly income is $70,000. This is the chart that they filled out, based on their financial situation.

NOTE: if your budget only allows $100 or $200 a month it will still work, it will just take longer. The higher your Power Payment, the faster you will get out of debt.

	1	2	3	4	5	6	7
	Debt	Total Owed	Minimum monthly payment	Column 2 ÷ Column 3	Priority	Power Payment	Months to pay off 2÷6
1	Mastercard	$3,150.00	$126.00	25	5	959+126= $1085	3
2	Mastercard	$8,200.00	$328.00	25	6	1085+328= $1413	6
3	Visa	$2,200.00	$76.00	25	4	883+76= $959	2
4	Discover	$800.00	$32.00	25	3	851+32= $883	1
5	Dept Store	$630.00	$26.00	25	2	825+26= $851	1
6	Car 1	$10,200.00	$425.00	24	1	400+425= $825	12
7	Car 2	$15,000.00	$480.00	31	7	1413+480= $1893	8
8	Heloc	$30,000.00	$350.00	86	8	1893+350= $2243	14
9	Mortgage	$150,000.00	$1,079.00	128	9	2243+1079= $3322	45
	Total	$220,180				Total	92

How to fill it out:

- On the first column of your chart, write down the accounts in which you have outstanding balances.

- On column #2, write down the current balance. On column #3, enter the minimum monthly payment.

- On column #4, divide column #2 by column #3, and enter the resulting number here. This will be the approximate number of months that it will take you to pay off the loan by paying only the minimum payment. The amount is NOT exact but it's here only to determine the order in which you will be paying off your accounts. Now look at this column and look for the lowest number; this will be the account you will pay off first. For credit cards, please note that banks usually require a minimum payment equal to 2% to 4% of your balance (there are exceptions); that's why in this example the number is 25 for all credit cards on column #4. If this is your case and you also have more than one account with the same number, just focus on the account with the lowest balance FIRST.

- On column # 5, enter the priority based on column #4, lowest numbers first.

- Now, column #6 is where you will enter, for your first account (in this example, the one highlighted on column #5), your "Power Payment" + the minimum payment for that account. In this case it would be $435 (minimum payment) + $400 (Power Payment) = $835 total payment. Now this account will be paid off in just over 12 months.

Then proceed to send the minimum payment to all accounts, and the minimum + your Power Payment to your #1 account (on column 5) until this account is paid off. Once it is paid off, then you are going to target account #2 (also on column 5), adding your Power Payment + the minimum payment you were sending before to your first account. In this example, for account #2, it would be $835 ($400 Power Payment + $435 minimum payment you were sending before to account #1, now paid off) + $27 (minimum payment for account #2). Keep working this plan until all accounts are paid off. You will get out of debt, all accounts paid off (including your mortgage) in record time! How will you feel once you are debt-free?

Let it Multiply!
A few things you can do that will help you with your plan:

- Put your debt elimination chart in a place where you can see it often

- As soon as an account is paid off, use a red marker and cross it off, or write PAID OFF (and the DATE) in big, red letters

- Also, every time you pay off an account, go celebrate! Take your spouse (or significant other) out to dinner and feel the power of your determination and persistence.

- As you see the progress you are making on your chart, think (with emotion) "I am becoming debt-free". Feel how it feels to be debt free. Pat yourself on the shoulder for a job well done! (Do it, it works!)

- Remember that extreme situations require extreme solutions and sacrifices, so if you need to, work extra hours, get a second job, hold garage sales, sell stuff you can live without, unsubscribe from services you don't really need, etc. If your car is paid off, resist the temptation to buy another one (for as long as possible). You get the idea.

- Make sure your savings account has at least $2000 as an emergency fund. Add any extra money you can to your Power Payment and to your savings, but do not withdraw from your savings except for an emergency. If you do, replenish it ASAP.

- Every day, several times a day, and say to yourself: "I am wealth, I am abundance, I am health, and I am joy". Feel it deep inside, feel the abundance surrounding you. This was taken from an excellent book called "A happy pocket full of money". Or pick a phrase you believe in, and repeat it to yourself, with feelings, several times a day like a mantra.

Remember, keeping up with the Jones' (other people who are in debt) will only make you a slave to debt for life. Now you know you can control your debt. Once you start your debt elimination plan, you will feel the power that comes from being in control of your finances. You can live your life by design and create a bright future for yourself and your family.

Now that you understand the step-by-step plan to get out of debt, commit yourself to doing it. You deserve to be debt-free!

CHAPTER 7- ASK FOR PROFESSIONAL HELP TO CONTROL YOUR SPENDING HABITS

There seems to be a widespread misconception about what a credit counselor can and cannot do for you, so let's start by explaining what Credit Counseling is and then we'll explain what Debt Settlement is.

Credit Counselors will not settle your debts that are not what they do. What they can do for you is consolidate your unsecured debts and lower your interest rates, and then collect a payment from you through a debt management plan.

Credit Counseling, when done through a reputable company, can be a great help to get out of debt. It is also known as Debt Consolidation since the idea is to consolidate all your unsecured debts into one account, and you send only one payment every month to the Credit Counseling company who in turn forwards it to your creditors. They usually charge a fee of about $35-$60 per month for their services and you can expect to be debt free within 5 years. They will negotiate a lower rate for you (about 7-9 % or so, depending on several factors) which can sometimes be a huge reduction (keep in mind that some people are paying 23% or more!). When you start the process, you will be asked to cut up your credit cards which is always a good thing to do when you are in debt (regardless of whether you do debt consolidation or not!)

You will probably not be able to get new credit until your accounts are paid off (let's face it, who would give you credit if they see in your credit report that you haven't been able to pay the other creditors?) but the great thing is that you know you can be debt free in a few short years.

A good credit counseling company will do what its name implies, they will teach you how to handle your finances, and many will even offer financial classes to help you understand how to manage your money properly.

The challenge is that many credit counseling agencies may not have your best interest in mind. I know this for a fact, since I once started working for a Credit Counseling company in San Diego and had to resign on my second day when I became aware of their unethical practices. I simply would never be part of a company that takes advantage of the people it is supposed to be helping. I told the owner what I thought and resigned; it was clear to me that he was in that business just for the money (and he was making A LOT of it!).

Debt settlement, on the other hand, is when a creditor forgives a portion of your debt if they think that they will not be able to collect the total amount. The reasoning is simple: it's better to collect something than nothing.

Let it Multiply!

Obviously not everybody will be able to settle their debts. A person may be successful settling one debt but maybe another credit card may not be willing to settle. If you can convince them with enough facts that you absolutely cannot pay the entire amount, they you have a very good chance of reaching a good settlement.

Since a credit card settlement will show up as a negative on your credit report, this option is not for you if you are paying your bills on time, have a good record and would like to keep it that way.

Please note that debt settlement should ONLY be used as a last resource if you are considering bankruptcy; the process can sometimes be difficult and its effectiveness will depend on many factors. It's like doing your own taxes. Yes, you can do it, but you will never know how much better would have been if it was done by a professional. Almost always it would be done much better by a professional.

I strongly suggest that if you decide to go this route and decide to try to settle your debts, you hire a professional to do the job for you. This way you will be way ahead of the game, since a professional has been through the process many times and has the experience necessary to reach a good settlement agreement on your behalf.

Keep in mind that collectors are people who have been trained to collect money; they do it every day for a living, so they do know what they are doing. They are used to negotiating with people, and they have been through different scenarios and situations. So the best option is to hire somebody who is used to dealing with these trained collectors and knows how to play their game.

Just be very careful since there are a lot of crooks out there it's always better to go with a company or attorney that was referred to you by somebody who can give you good references about their services.

But if you do decide to do it yourself, here are some guidelines that will help you achieve very good results.

1- Settling will only work if your account is seriously past due. Companies will only offer a good settlement option when they believe it's their last chance to recover their money. When they think that if they don't settle, they won't recover a penny of the money you owe. Usually, the best time to start negotiating a debt settlement is about 4 or 5 months after you sent your last payment. Remember that at about 6 months or less they will probably sell your account to a collection agency, so do not wait for more than 5 months. Once the account is sold to the collection agency, you will lose most of your leverage. You can still settle, but it's not the same, the sense of "urgency" that the credit card company had before is now lost.

2- Most settlements are for between 30 and 70% of the amount owed. It will depend on several factors, mostly on your negotiation skills and how long it has been since you sent your last payment. You may want to offer 20%, but expect your offer to be rejected. Your goal should be to settle for about 50% of your debt, but settling for 2/3rds can be a reasonable goal. Keep in mind that people who actually settle for 10-20% are the exception to the rule; very few people accomplish this.

3- Before you talk to them, make sure you have all the paperwork you need in front of you:

-all copies of your statements, letters from your creditors, and a dedicated notepad where you can take notes of everything you discuss during your conversation. Remember to always write down the date and time of the call, the name of the person you talked to, their number or extension if they can provide it, and everything you talked about.

4- This is one of the most critical factors here: always, no matter what they say and how much they threaten you, ALWAYS be nice to them. Never, EVER use profane language or threats; it will only make you lose your battle. The key is to always be nice and treat them with respect. If you deviate from this even for a moment, you lose.

5- Make sure you get all offers in writing. Whatever you talk on the phone, if you don't get it in writing, is useless. Anytime they offer a deal you find acceptable, make sure you ask them to send it to you in writing.

6- Occasionally you may talk to somebody who might not be willing to negotiate, or who will treat you in a disrespectful way. In this case, you can either politely terminate the call, or ask to speak to a supervisor. But again, always be very polite and respectful, and never use profane language or threats.

7- Ask them to remove all late fees, finance charges and over the limit fees from your account. This alone will reduce your balance substantially. Do not demand, always ask politely. "You know, I would really like to pay you all that I owe, but I simply can't. I lost my job and have very limited income (or whatever your situation is). But if we can get the balance to be more manageable for me, I am willing to start sending you payments starting this week". If they see that you are sincere and willing to pay them, you have more chances that they will be willing to help you.

8- You will be talking (mostly) to trained professionals. They go through extensive training on how to collect money and how to ask the right questions to get the information they want. So never lie to them. Just be sincere, you want to pay but you don't have the means, but if they can help you by reducing the total balance you will be happy to pay them. This is the attitude that will help you.

9- Always start with a goal in mind. What would be a good amount to settle for? Say you owe $10,000 to a credit card company. A good number would be $5,000 (50%) or less, but it will depend on many factors. So if they offer you to settle for $8,000 you can politely decline, because it would "probably" be better just to file bankruptcy (again, if they feel they will lose it all because you are filing for bankruptcy, they may concede). Many times you will get a phone call or a letter a few days later offering to settle for less.

10- Keep in mind that they will almost always run your credit report and look at your payment history. So if you are paying all your bills on time but not to XYZ Company, then XYZ will not be willing to settle with you. After all, if you are paying everybody else, chances are you can pay them as well. But if they see in your report that you have not been paying most of your bills for over three months, or four months, then they will most likely be willing to settle with you. If they see it's their last chance to recover their money, then you have leverage. But this is a two-edge sword as it can backfire on you if you don't know how to negotiate properly.

11- There are four factors critical to the success of the debt-settlement negotiation process: Communicating effectively, Negotiating, Documenting and Following Up. When you excel in all four you will walk away with great results.

12- When you agree to send a payment, many times the collector will ask you to pay right then, while you are on the phone. It is very important that you do not do so: make sure they send you the offer in writing FIRST; then you mail them the check. You can say something like this: "I understand you want a payment right now, but unfortunately I cannot make a payment at this time, it is just not possible. I will have $_____ soon and want to settle at least one of my accounts with whoever will give me the best deal. Could you please send me an offer in writing?" The amount you mention in your conversation should be a round number representing about 30-50% of your balance, or whatever you can pay at the time.

13- This is worth repeating many times, because it's critical to your success. Always be kind, nice and polite. Be sincere and never lie. Even though many collectors will not care, make sure they understand your situation. "I would love to pay you but I have been (laid off, in the hospital, with a reduced salary, got divorced, etc). I am desperate and I'm seriously considering filing for bankruptcy".

14- Every time you send them anything (whether a letter or a payment) use Certified Mail with return receipt. Remember that documentation is extremely important; it is one of the four factors that will determine how successful you are.

So this is the debt settlement process. It is not hard, but most people will probably have better results if they go with a trained professional. If you do decide to do it yourself, make sure you read this chapter several times, leave nothing to chance and do your research first! Study the steps & write down what you are going to tell them.

CHAPTER 8- FRUGAL LIVING EASILY ACHIEVED WITH POSITIVE THINKING

The Psychology of Money – Changing your mindset

"Whatever you believe with emotion becomes your reality. You always act in a manner consistent with your innermost beliefs and convictions"

Brian Tracy

I am convinced that this part of the book is more important than the step-by-step plan we have just described. To me, it doesn't make sense to show you how to get out of debt unless you can change your mind set about what is possible for you. Once you change your mindset and you get out of debt, nothing can stop you.

I found that most of the times when we fail to achieve what we really want, there is an underlying belief (that we are usually not aware of) that is not supporting us. Have you ever experienced self-sabotage? Have you ever failed to follow through on something that you wanted to achieve? Most likely you had conflicting beliefs that were pulling you in different directions.

But what is a belief? A belief is a feeling of certainty about what something means to you. Most of our beliefs are generalizations about our past that are based on interpretations of our experiences. In other words, they are based on how we interpreted what happened to us at the moment. Let me give you an example.

Twin brothers go to an amusement park and decide to take a ride on a roller-coaster together. One walks out of that ride feeling very happy and thrilled, and these effects will be positive over his lifetime. The other, however, walks out of that same ride full of fear and shock, and those effects will be negative for him over his lifetime. It was the same ride, but it was perceived differently by them. We all perceive and interpret our experiences in a different way.

Which brings me to another very important point that you should always remember: it is not what happens to us in life, but how we interpret what happens to us and what we decide to focus on that changes our life. We need to take responsibility for where we are in life, feel grateful for it and move on.

Blaming our situation or our "conditions" will only bring more of the same. By feeling grateful for what you have, whatever that may be, you are actually impressing thoughts of abundance upon the Universe, and the Universe will deliver to you more abundance. It may sound strange to some people, but it is one of the immutable Laws of the Universe, the Law of Attraction. For more information on the Law of Attraction, see the Resources section.

But let's go back to your beliefs and how they affect your life. They actually affect everything you do, since all your actions are the result of your beliefs. They are extremely important to achieving success in anything you do.

You see, from the day we are born we are bombarded with negative suggestions. Not knowing how to counter them, we unconsciously accept them and bring them into being as our experience.

For example, we are told:

- You cannot do it / You can't do that

- if you don't wear a sweater, you will catch a cold

- You don't have a chance

- Things are only getting worse

- You may get fired

- You are not smart enough

And so on. Get the idea?

Consider now the fact that right now in America, there are about 36 million people that are 65 years of age and older. Out of that 36 million people, over 34 million are broke. They are depending on someone else for life's necessities.

Why is it that in the richest country in the world, 95% of the population ends up broke?

Let it Multiply!

If you ask these people, they would tell you that their lives were shaped by exterior forces or circumstances, by things that happened to them. This implies that they were not in control, that they were merely a leaf in the wind.

But as we said before, and it's so important that it is worth repeating, it is not what happens to us in life, but how we interpret what happens to us and what we decide to focus on that changes our life. A person's fortune can be completely wiped out, and he or she can build it again with the right mindset. It has happened millions of times, which proves that it is NOT what happens to you but how you react to it.

The main reason that most people never achieve financial independence is that we are not taught how to succeed. We are not taught how to achieve financial independence. We are not taught how to handle money. We are never taught that WE are in charge of our lives.

The educational system in place today was created in the 1800's, and was designed to prepare us to work as employees. In high school, we are not taught how to handle money, how to invest it, how to create passive streams of income. We don't learn it either in College or University. We grow up (most of us, anyway) believing that money is in short supply, is hard to come by and that you have to work really hard for it. We grow up associating different things to money like "If I have a lot of money, I may lose my friends," thereby, "money equals loneliness." Other common beliefs are "money changes people, they become greedy", "If I make a lot of money, I could lose my motivation". Or, "If I'm broke (or poor) people will pay more attention to me". And the list goes on and on.

The fact is that money by itself is neither good or bad. It is what we associate to money that makes all the difference in the world.

Let me give you a few examples that affected me personally.

I lived most of my life under a set of beliefs that controlled most of what I did. It took me a while to identify those beliefs, but when I did, I realized that they had such an enormous power over me that they controlled my focus, my ideas, and my acts. Before I was aware of these beliefs, I blamed my circumstances on other people or "bad luck".

When I was growing up, money was always tight. My father lost his job when I was 8 years old. He could never get another job that paid him enough, so we were always short of money. My parents had no choice but to take me out of private school and send me to public school. I remember my parents saying to me, "we are middle class", and as a kid, I accepted it as if it were a fact that would never change.

Growing up in an environment of lack, I felt that money was in short supply. That money only went to other people richer than me. People said that "money can't buy you happiness", and I believed it. I deeply believed that because of circumstances that were beyond my control, other people could have money, but not me. I believed I was "middle class", period. I was "destined" to be that way.

Let me ask you, how do you think living with these beliefs affected my life as an adult? How did it affect what was possible or impossible for me?

At a conscious level, I wanted to earn a lot of money so I could live comfortably. But deep inside me, (at a subconscious level) I never believed I could earn good money. When I worked as a salesperson many years ago, I would have a great week, and then during the next 3 weeks I would sabotage my own success. I would not work hard until the money ran out. This was done subconsciously of course; there was always a "reasonable" excuse for not working hard.

I am very grateful to the Universe for the parents I have and the experiences I had, since they prepared me for what I am today.

The truth of the matter is that all beliefs that we "inherit" from our parents, are beliefs that they "inherited" from their parents.

So I now choose to believe things that will inspire me, and I do not really care if they are factual truths or not; they will become truths once I believe in them.

A couple of examples of my new beliefs are:

- I am a soul with a body; my soul is infinitely abundant

- I am always surrounded by abundance. Abundance is all there is.

- Money always comes easily and effortlessly

- I am wealth – I am abundance – I am health

You have beliefs about everything. And what is great about identifying and changing your beliefs, is that you can choose to believe anything that can help you achieve your goals.

You have to look for those limiting beliefs that are controlling your life. If you are ready to break free from the chains of limiting beliefs, I will guide you through a simple yet very powerful process that will enable you to change those beliefs for good.

You can literally change anything you want.

To get the best results out of the following exercise, you will need a quiet place and privacy.

If you are in debt, you need to adopt new beliefs that will empower you. You can decide what you will choose to believe, so why not find beliefs that will help you achieve your goals? Beliefs that limit your actions can be as devastating as positive beliefs can be empowering. When we fully believe something is true, it is like delivering a command to our brain as to how to represent what is occurring. In other words, they are "filters" to our perceptions of the world.

We need to take responsibility for where we are in life. We need to stop blaming others for what happens to us, and decide to move forward.

A few good beliefs to have are:

1- Everything happens for a good reason (even if, right now, I cannot see what that good reason is)

2- People are inherently good

3- Money is easy to come by

4- The Universe is abundant and limitless, and money never runs out

5- Even before a problem occurs, it has already been solved. There is a solution to it somewhere, and I will find it.

6- I am wealth – I am abundance – I am health

Let it Multiply!

7- I am a spirit with a body; my spirit is eternally abundant and wealthy

8- Being broke is only temporary.

Feel free to come up with any beliefs that will empower you, in all areas of your life.

There are several ways to change beliefs on purpose. The following method is the one I found to be the most effective. It involves associating a lot of emotional pain to the old belief, and a lot of emotional pleasure to the new belief. This is a process you do only once for the belief to be replaced with an empowering one of your choice.

Now let's start the process of changing our old beliefs. Let me warn you though, that just reading this exercise will not change anything in your life! You DO NEED to complete this exercise. Believe me, it will be fun, and it will not take long. And you can do it as many times as you want, any time you discover a belief that is not empowering you.

A way to identify a belief is this: they are usually found after the word "because", on phrases you usually say. As an example, if you hear yourself saying something like, "I will always be fat, because my father and mother are overweight, and I have their genes". Another example, "They wouldn't give me that job, because I am not smart enough". Or, "I could never succeed, because I never succeeded before in my life". Do you get the idea?

Let's start with your limiting beliefs. Write down 5 beliefs that you have about yourself and what you are capable of. What are five beliefs that have limited you in the past? i.e., "I could never make more than $50,000 a year", "I can't get a better job", "nobody would pay me that much", etc.

1_____

2_____

3_____

4_____

5_____

Now you write down 5 empowering beliefs that can now support you in achieving your goals. Do not limit yourself in your new beliefs. Think big, think bold! Also, and this is extremely important, state your beliefs in the affirmative, never state a belief that negates what you don't want. Example: "My life is abundant" is a great example, but "I don't have any more debt" is not, since it is not positive enough, and your brain will focus on "debt" instead of the "I don't". These new beliefs will replace the ones that have limited you before.

1_____

2_____

3_____

4_____

5_____

Let it Multiply!

Excellent! Feel grateful for taking this first step that can change your life for the better.

Now, get two pieces of paper. On the first piece of paper, write down the first limiting belief you are eliminating. What you are going to do first is create doubt. Once you start to doubt a belief, it becomes weak, making it easier to replace with another belief. Then, you are going to associate massive pain to having that belief, and massive pain in the future if you continue to have that belief. In other words, you have to feel the negative emotions associated with living with that belief, and how it would negatively affect you. Then, on the other piece of paper, you are going to associate massive pleasure to the new belief that you want to adopt in its place.

This exercise is extremely powerful, so please, do yourself a favor and take it seriously. You can change your life now.

Let's start with the first belief. You have already written this belief down on the first piece of paper; now ask yourself the following questions:

1- How is this belief ridiculous or absurd?

2- What negative consequences have you already experienced as a result of having this RIDICULOUS belief? What has it cost you emotionally, financially, physically and in your relationships in the past, because of having this ABSURD belief?

3- What is it costing you now, emotionally, financially, physically and in your relationships, because of having this WRONG belief?

4- What will it cost you emotionally, financially, physically, in your relationships, during the next 10 years, if you don't let go of this belief now?

Write down everything that comes to your mind. Keep writing about all the pain you experienced in your past, all the pain you are experiencing right now, and all the pain you will be experiencing in the future if you don't change this absurd belief now.

Make sure you feel as much pain as possible. Feel all the negative emotions associated with having this absurd belief. Close your eyes and visualize it, live it, feel it as if it were happening right now. I know this doesn't sound very appealing, but believe me; you will be amazed at the results!

Once you are fully associated with the pain that having this belief has cost you and would have cost you your whole life, get the second piece of paper, and write down the new empowering belief that will take the place of the old one.

Ask yourself the following questions:

1- How will having this empowering belief affect my life?

2- What benefits will I get from having this empowering belief?

3- How will I feel and how will I act by having this empowering belief?

4- Where will I be in 10 years as a result of having this empowering belief?

Let it Multiply!

5- Imagine yourself 10 years from now, and looking back at the last 10 years, how does it feel having lived with this empowering belief? Stay there for a while, feeling those great feelings.

While you are writing down each answer, make sure you fully associate with the positive feelings of having this empowering belief. Feel how much better your life is as a result of having this belief. Close your eyes and feel it in your body. How would you feel? How would you move? How would you breathe?

The key here is to experience as much pleasure as possible.

Now grab the first piece of paper containing your old beliefs, and burn it. As you see the paper burning, feel the old belief vanishing in your past, and feel the power of your new belief.

Congratulations! Feel grateful for having a great, empowering belief that will support you for the rest of your life.

Do the same with the next belief, and keep repeating until you finish replacing all your old beliefs.

This exercise was adapted from similar exercises by Anthony Robbins and Bob Proctor.

Another way to replace limiting beliefs

I recently found another way to change beliefs and counter negative suggestions that I use very frequently. It is incredibly powerful and it also helps me to keep focused on what I want.

Even though I used affirmations in the past, they never seemed to work for me. Throughout the years I heard about how important it was to repeat to yourself the "right" affirmations, and since I never noticed any benefits I quit doing it.

But it wasn't until I watched the movie "You can heal your life" by Louis Hayes that I finally "got it". In the movie, a person who got cured of cancer explained that she was repeating an affirmation 400 times a day. Four hundred times a day! That's why it worked for her; her subconscious mind ended up believing what she was affirming. It never worked for me because I would repeat my affirmations only a few times a day (no wonder, right?)

So one day I found a cheap Mardi Gras bead necklace that was given to me at a party and I thought to myself: "This would be great to use while I practice my affirmations". It has 88 beads, so I would repeat one affirmation out loud about 100 times while I was going through the necklace on my way to work every morning, with emotion and feeling it as if it was already real. Then, on my way back home, I would repeat the process. It was a total of about 200 affirmations a day, but I wanted to find a way to double that.

So what I did was to shorten the affirmations without modifying their meaning, and also to write them down whenever I could. Their benefits were incredible! It took about three weeks to start seeing the benefits, but then I got hooked. I would do one affirmation for at least three weeks before moving on to the next one.

The best way I found is to start the affirmations with "I'm so happy and grateful now that…" and fill in the blanks with whatever you want to achieve or get. Some examples could be:

"I'm so happy and grateful now that I'm driving my …. (name/model of car you want)"

Let it Multiply!

"I'm so happy and grateful now that I get up at 5:00 AM fully energized"

"I'm so happy and grateful now that I weigh 175 lbs (or whatever you want)"

"I'm so happy and grateful now that my Chase MasterCard is fully paid off"

"I'm so happy and grateful now that money comes easily and frequently"

Write down a list of affirmations and pick one to start with. Repeat your affirmation out loud, 200 to 400 times a day. It's Ok to try different tones of voice since you will probably get tired after a while. I found that it works ten times better to say them out loud than in your head, so say them out loud as many times as possible.

How to use affirmations effectively

In his book, "The spiritual basis of real prosperity", Roy Eugene Davis says about affirmations:

"Mechanical repetition of affirmations is a waste of time. Speak with deliberate, soul-felt conviction until super conscious awareness of the reality of that which is affirmed is clear and unwavering". In other words, live the affirmation as if it were true, with deep emotion and conviction (excellent book to read by the way).

At the beginning it will probably feel weird and your brain may go: "liar, you know this is not true!" but keep going. After a while, your subconscious mind will start accepting it. And once your subconscious mind believes it, your life will start to change.

Changing your mindset

Remember what the definition of insanity is? Doing the same thing over and over and expecting a different result.

If you want things to change, YOU have to change first. You can be in control of your life by choosing what to focus on most of the time.

Successful people choose to focus on positive things; unsuccessful people focus on negative things by default.

So do what successful people do:

• Spend most of your time focusing on positive things, NOT on negative things.

• Focus on what you want to achieve, NOT on what you do not want to achieve.

• Focus on what you like, NOT on what you don't like.

Before I learned this lesson I would curse every fault of the car I owned at the time. The more I focused on it, the more miserable I felt. When I learned to be thankful for the car, I changed my mindset and I felt better.

I am not saying to ignore your problems. Acknowledge your problems, but don't dwell on them.

Be thankful for the problem since, most likely, it is an opportunity in disguise. You can find the greatest opportunities of your life "hidden" in your worst moments. That's why all successful people see problems as opportunities.

Let it Multiply!

The best advice I can give you is to reframe every "difficulty". That means that you find the good in a seemingly "bad" situation.

Always focus on abundance, not lack or problems. Focus on wealth building, not surviving. Focus on your next check, not your last one.

When you find yourself thinking about the negative aspects of your life, immediately replace the negative thoughts with a positive one, like a mantra. If you catch yourself saying, "I can't afford it," immediately say "I couldn't afford it in the past, but I can afford it now. I just choose not to buy it at this time," or something similar. You don't have to believe it yet. You can "fake it 'til you make it."

Feel abundance in your life and be grateful for your abundance. What you focus on expands. If you focus on lack, it expands. When you focus on abundance, it expands as well.

Remember, abundance isn't just about money. You may have an abundance of friends, health, faith or ideas. Look at nature. Everywhere you turn there is abundance. Life, by its very nature, is abundant. Just open your eyes; open your mind.

Of course this is easier said than done, so how to start?

There are several things you can do right away:

1- Start meditating every day. Even if you don't know how to meditate, at least find a quiet spot, sit comfortably, close your eyes, and breathe deeply. Focus on your breathing. Stay like this for a few minutes, and avoid any thoughts; just focus on your breathing. Then visualize a goal you want to achieve, and feel as if you have already achieved it. FEEL what it feels like to have achieved that goal. Make it as real as possible. Touch it, feel it, smell it, see it. Stay in that feeling for a few minutes, and thank the

Universe for having achieved it. This is probably the most powerful exercise you can do to become successful.

2- Read positive books, every single day. At least read for 15 minutes, preferably for 30 minutes or more. I always read before going to bed, so I can go to sleep with positive thoughts and feelings.

3- Listen to positive CDs in your car instead of music (or what's worse, the news!)

4- Avoid the news, negative people, negative movies, negative talk shows and anything that will affect you negatively. Feed your mind with positive things every day.

5- Feel genuinely grateful for what you have. FEEL deep feelings of gratitude. This is incredibly powerful, so do not take it lightly. Feel grateful for anything you have, your car (even if you don't like it, still feel grateful for having it), your kids, your spouse, a flower, etc. Feel grateful every day. Write down a list of things you are grateful for, and as you are writing, feel the gratitude. Do it for 5-10 minutes every day. Make sure that as soon as you wake up, you think about things to be grateful for. It's the best way to start your day!

6- Surround yourself with positive people that inspire you. This is very important! One way could be to start a mastermind group, where all of you can share ideas and support each other. You can either meet at somebody's house once a week or at a restaurant. You can even do a conference call once a week if some of you live in different cities. You can also find a mentor that can help you stay focused or new friends that share the same goals.

Let it Multiply!

7- Feel the abundance that surrounds you. Even if at this moment you don't have the money you want, you can find abundance if you look for it. Abundance is not just money; abundance is everywhere. Maybe you have an abundance of love? Or an abundance of friends? Look for abundance in Nature. Look at the ocean, you will see abundance. Look at trees, you will see abundance. Just FEEL abundance instead of lack and you will attract it.

8- Take workshops when possible, take classes if you can. Find an Adult School. Their classes are free.

You can make your life a masterpiece. Just focus on it, every day. And always, ALWAYS, be grateful for what you have.

There is NOTHING that you cannot be, do, or have. You are a magnificent human being with unlimited potential. Do not settle for mediocrity, you deserve more.

About The Author

Nolan Myers is a well-known entrepreneur and a financial analyst in East Coast. He started his coffee shop business on his early twenties and it easily grows big with the dedication and skills that Nolan possesses. Nolan Myers is often invited in different businesses to give his ideas on how to increase revenue and lessen expenses.

Nolan Myers lives in NY with his family.